I0510208

COPYRIGHT

CONTENTS

"This book is dedicated to Terraine and Shaquanna for putting up with my "ways" and of course my children, family and friends as well as all Dreamers..."

INTRODUCTION

Building a good credit score, also known as a credit rating, is crucial because it can affect your ability to borrow money or access products such as credit cards or loans. You can check your score for free and if it isn't in the best shape, there are things you can do to improve it.

Your credit score is created from information held in your credit report, also known as your credit file.

The exact number of your credit score can differ between lenders or even between different products from the same lender, depending on the criteria used in assessing you as a potential customer.

The information held on your credit file and your credit application form might be used to decide:

- whether to lend to you
- how much to let you borrow
- how much interest to charge you.

The most recent information on your file will have the most impact, as lenders will be most interested in your current financial situation. That said, your financial decisions, good or bad, from the last six years, will still be on record.

If your credit report shows a few missed payments, you might be charged higher interest by lenders or might not be eligible for some loans.

This is because lenders believe they might be taking a higher risk when lending to you.

Your credit history can affect your ability to get things like insurance or begin mobile phone contracts. Regularly checking your report is a great idea, because it can help you spot any fraudulent activity or mistakes on your report.

You might think bad credit only keeps you from getting a credit card or loan, but it goes further than that. Bad credit can leave you homeless, carless, and jobless. That's because more and more businesses are using your credit to make decisions about you. Still not convinced it's time to get your credit act together?

NEW HOPE CREDIT SOLUTIONS LLC will tutor your path to a successful credit solution.

22 WAYS TO IMPROVE YOUR CREDIT SCORE RIGHT NOW

A good credit score is a little like a professional network: You care about it only when you really need it.

A good credit score can mean qualifying for lower interest rates and better terms; a bad one can mean you don't ☐ualify for any kind of financing at all.

Unfortunately, if you need to borrow money -- or get insurance, or lease a facility, or build inventory, or a variety of other reasons -- and you don't have a good credit score, it's impossible to correct the situation overnight. That's why the time to start repairing your credit is now, not when you really need it.

Fortunately improving your credit score is easy.

Here's how...

1. Check out your credit reports.

The credit bureaus -- TransUnion, E☐uifax, and Experian -- are re☐uired to give you a free copy of your report once a year. All you have to do is ask.

Another way to see your credit reports is to use a service like Credit Karma. (I'm not specifically endorsing Credit Karma: I like it and think it's handy, but I'm sure other free services are useful too. Unlike some services, Credit Karma is free and you don't have to provide credit card information.)

Once you've signed up, you can see your TransUnion and E☐uifax credit scores and view the information contained on those reports. Generally speaking the entries on the different reports will be the same, but not always; for a variety of reasons credit reports are rarely identical.

2. Dispute derogatory marks.

In the old days, you had to write letters to the credit bureaus if you wanted to dispute errors. Services like Credit Karma let you do it online.

Just make sure you get the most bang for your dispute bucks. Certain factors weigh more heavily on your credit score than others, so pay attention to them first.

We'll start with derogatory marks like collection accounts and judgments. It's not uncommon to have at least one collection account appear on your report. I had two from health care providers I used after having a severe panic attack; my insurance company was extremely slow to pay and kept claiming it had paid while the providers said it had not, and eventually the accounts ended up with a collection agency. At that point, I decided to pay them right away and argue with the insurance company later, but both collections wound up on my credit report.

Fixing those problems was easy. I clicked the "dispute" button that appeared by the account, selected "The creditor agreed to remove my liability on this account," and within a week the dispute was resolved and the entry was removed from my credit report.

You can also dispute errors through each credit bureau (I did it through Credit Karma). If that's your preference, go here for TransUnion, here for E☐uifax, and here for Experian.

Keep in mind some disputes will take longer than others. But that's Ok -- once you initiate a dispute, you're done. The credit bureaus are re☐uired to investigate the dispute and report the resolution.

Spend as much time as it takes trying to have derogatory marks removed because they also weigh heavily on your overall score. Then...

3. Dispute late payments.

Mistakes happen. Your mortgage lender may report that a payment was late that was in fact paid on time. A credit card provider may fail to enter a payment correctly.

You can dispute late payments -- whether in accounts that are current or accounts that have been closed -- the same way you dispute derogatory marks.

Your payment history is another factor that weighs heavily on your credit score, so work hard to clean up errors.

4. Decide how far you're willing to go.

So far we've discussed trying to remove inaccurate information only. You can, if you choose, also dispute accurate information.

For example, say an account went to collection, you never paid it, and the collection agency gave up. All that remains is the entry on your credit report. You can still choose to dispute the entry. Many people do. And sometimes those entries will get removed.

Why? When you enter a dispute the credit bureau asks the creditor to verify the information. Some will. Many, like collection agencies, will not. They'll simply ignore the re☐uest

-- and if they do ignore the re□uest, the agency is re□uired to remove the entry from your credit report.

What that means is that smaller firms, like collection agencies or local lenders or small to midsize service providers, are less likely to respond to the credit bureaus. It's a hassle they don't need. Banks, credit card companies, auto finance companies, and mortgage lenders are a lot more likely to respond.

So if you want -- and I'm not recommending this; I'm just saying it's a strategy you might decide to use -- you can dispute information that you think is accurate in hopes that the creditor will not respond. (This is the strategy many credit repair firms use to try to improve their clients' scores.) If the creditor doesn't respond, the entry will get removed.

Should you take this approach? That's up to you. (You could argue I shouldn't even mention it, but it is something people do, so I felt it was worth discussing.)

5. Do a little haggling.

Maybe you tried and failed to remove a negative comment, or a late payment, or an account that was marked "paid as agreed" (which might mean the creditor agreed to let you pay less than you owed). Should you give up? Nope. Try asking nicely.

Creditors can tell credit bureaus to remove entries from your credit report at any time. For example, I hadn't charged anything on a particular credit card for months and didn't notice that I had been charged my annual fee until the payment was late. (Like a doofus, I was just tossing the bills unopened because I "knew" there were no charges.)

The late payment showed up on my credit report so I called the credit card company, explained what had happened, said I had been a customer for years, and asked if they would remove the entry. They said sure. And they also agreed to waive all annual fees in the future. (Proving yet again that you can't get if you don't ask.)

When all else fails, call and ask nicely. You'll be surprised by how often a polite re☐uest for help pays off.

6. Increase your credit limits.

Another factor that weighs heavily on your credit score is credit card utilization. Your ratio of available credit to credit used makes a big difference. Generally speaking carrying a balance of more than 50 percent of your available credit will negatively impact your score; maxing out your cards will definitely hurt your score.

One way to improve your ratio is to pay down your balances, but another way is to increase your credit limit. If you owe $2,500 on a card with a $5,000 limit and you get the limit increased to $7,500, your ratio instantly improves.

How do you get your limits increased? Once again, call and ask nicely. If you have a decent payment history most credit card companies will be more than happy to increase your limit -- after all, they want you to carry a high balance. That's how they make money.

7. Get a new credit card.

Another way to increase your credit card utilization ratio is to get a new card. As long as you don't carry a balance on that card, your available credit immediately increases by that card's limit.

Try to get a card that doesn't charge an annual fee, though. Your best bet is through a bank where you already have an account. Granted cards with no annual fee tend to charge higher interest rates, but if you never carry a balance the interest rate is irrelevant.

But be smart about it; the goal isn't to get access to more cash, the goal is to improve your credit score. If you think you'll be tempted to run up a balance on a new card, don't get it.

8. Pay down your balances.

I know. You need a higher credit score because you want to borrow money; if you had the money to pay down your balances, then you might not need to borrow. Still: decreasing your percentage of available credit used can make a quick and significant impact on your credit score. So go on a bare-bones budget to free up cash to pay down your balance. Or sell something.

Paying down balances may be tough to pull off as a short-term move to increase your credit score, but it should be part of your long-term financial plan. Not only will your credit score increase over time, you won't pay as much interest -- which, if you think about it, is just giving the credit cards money you prefer to stay in your pocket.

9. Get added to another person's card.

Say your spouse has a credit card with little or no balance and a great payment history; if he or she agrees to add you as an authorized user on that account, from a credit score point of view you automatically benefit from her card's available credit as well as her payment history.

Keep in mind if he or she makes a late payment, that entry will appear as negative on your credit report too.

So choose your credit card friends wisely.

10. Hang on to your "old" credit cards.

Your age of credit history has a moderate but meaningful impact on your score. Say you've had a certain credit card for 10 years; closing that account will decrease your overall average credit history and can negatively impact your score, especially in the short term.

If you're hoping to increase your credit score but you also need to get rid of a credit card account, get rid of your "newest" card.

And finally, the one credit score gift guaranteed to keep on giving:

11. Pay all your bills on time.

Even one late payment can hurt your score. Do everything you can, from now on, to always pay your bills on time.

And if one month you aren't able to pay everything on time, be smart about which bills you pay late. Your mortgage lender or credit card provider will definitely report a late payment to the credit bureaus, but utilities and cell providers likely will not.

Check the "Accounts" section on your credit reports to see which accounts are listed, and if you have to pay late, choose an account that does not appear on your report.

And then work really hard to make sure you can always pay everything on time in the future. Your credit score will thank you, and so will your stress levels.

12. Stay on top of payments

Keep your debts in the green to show lenders you're responsible with credit.

According to Experian, payment history is the most influential factor for both FICO and VantageScore, the most common scoring systems.

Your credit score is essentially a reflection of your ability to pay back debts effectively. From a lender's perspective, an established history of timely payments is a good indicator you'll handle future debts responsibly, too.

"You want to avoid things like late payments, defaults, repossessions, foreclosures and third party collections," says John Ulzheimer, credit expert, formerly of FICO and Equifax. "And filing bankruptcy is a horrible idea. Anything that would indicate non-performance of a liability is going to harm your credit score."

Whats A Good Credit Score?

Find out which credit score □ualifies you for the best interest rates.

13. Keep tabs on your credit utilization rate

Weigh your balances relative to your credit limit to ensure you're not using too much available credit, a practice which can indicate risk.

"The higher that ratio, the fewer points you're going to earn in that category and your scores are absolutely going to suffer," Ulzheimer says.

Credit utilization is one of the most influential categories that influence your score. Your ideal rate may vary depending on the scoring system used.

"In FICO's systems, less than 10 percent is the optimal target," Ulzheimer says. "In fact, people who have the highest average FICO scores have a utilization of 7 percent." VantageScore, on the other hand, looks for a target utilization of 30 percent or below.

"I always default to 10 percent because that's going to keep you in the good zone for both of the scoring platforms," Ulzheimer says.

The date your revolving credit issuer reports your information to the credit bureaus may also impact your utilization rate.

According to Ulzheimer, FICO's scoring systems don't differentiate between those who pay in full each month and those who carry a balance; the utilization that appears when your issuer reports your account information is the rate scored. VantageScore, though, does consider whether you pay in full or carry your balance month to month.

If you struggle with high balances and mounting interest payments on your cards, consider consolidating with a zero percent introductory rate balance transfer credit card.

14. Leave old debts on your report

Once you finally get rid of student debt or pay off your auto loan, you may be impatient to get any trace of it wiped from your report.

But as long as your payments were timely and complete, those debt records may actually help your credit score. The same is true for you credit card accounts.

"An account that's paid in full is a good thing; however, closing an account isn't something that consumers should automatically do in the hopes that it will positively impact their credit score," says Nancy Bistritz-Balkan, vice president of communications and consumer education at E☐uifax. "Having an account with a long history and solid track record of paying bills on time, every time, are the types of responsible habits lenders and creditors look for."

Any bad debts that can impact your score negatively are automatically removed over time.

"Bankruptcies can stay on your report no longer than 10 years," Ulzheimer says. "Late payments and similar delinquencies like collections, repossessions, foreclosures and settlements, those are capped at seven years."

15. Take advantage of score-boosting programs

The number and average age of your accounts are both important factors in helping lenders determine how well you handle debt, which can leave those with a limited credit history at a disadvantage.

Experian Boost and UltraFICO are two programs that allow consumers to boost a thin credit profile with other financial information.

After opting into Experian Boost, you can connect your online banking data and allow the credit bureau add telecommunications and utility payment history to your report. UltraFICO allows you to give permission for your banking data, like checking and savings accounts, to be considered alongside your report when calculating your score.

16. Time your applications carefully

Every time you apply for a new line of credit, a hard inquiry is pulled on your report. This type of in□uiry lowers your score temporarily.

"In general, the effects of a hard in□uiry last anywhere from 6 to 12 months," a TransUnion representative tells Bankrate. "And that inquiry is only on your credit report for up to 24 months."

Research your likelihood of approval to ensure you're a good candidate before applying for a new credit card. You don't want to risk lowering your score for a denied application.

You should also refrain from applying for several credit cards within a short time frame or before taking out a large loan like a mortgage.

When you shop for a mortgage, auto or personal loan, you can keep hard inquiries to a minimum by making rate comparisons within a short time period.

Applications for the same type of loan within a designated time frame will only appear as a single hard inquiry. According to FICO, this span can vary from 14 to 45 days.

17. Be patient

You won't raise your credit score overnight, which is why one of the best ways to achieve an excellent score is to develop good long-term credit habits.

According to Ulzheimer, two influential factors that go into your score are the average age of information and the oldest account on your report.

"You're really going to need to have credit for a couple of decades before you max out those categories," Ulzheimer says. "It takes a really, really long time to improve a bad score and it takes a really short amount of time to trash a good score."

Establish good habits, like paying your balances on time, keeping a low utilization rate and applying for credit only when you need it, and you should see those practices reflected in your score over time.

18. Monitor your credit

When you view your own credit, a soft in☐uiry is pulled, which doesn't affect your credit temporarily the way hard inquiries do.

"The information in the credit reports will not only enable you to see all of your financial accounts in one place, but reviewing them may also help you spot signs of identity theft," Bisritz-Balkan says.

Monitoring your score's fluctuations every few months can help you understand how well you're managing your credit and whether you should make any changes.

According to Ulzheimer, "As long as you pay your bills on time and as long as you keep your credit card balances modest and as long as you only apply for credit when you need it, then you really have no choice but to have a good score."

19. Dispute errors...even the small ones

Your first step: Order a copy of all three credit reports from the major players – E□uifax, TransUnion, and Experian. Order your reports, print a copy, and start reviewing.

Look for the big errors first, things like accounts that don't belong to you, paid balances that are showing as unpaid, and credit limits that are reported incorrectly. Highlight each one of these errors and then dispute them with the credit bureau. You can file a dispute online through each of the credit bureaus' websites:

E□uifax: Online Dispute

Experian: Dispute Your Credit Report Online

TransUnion: Initiate a Dispute on Your Credit Profile

After I disputed the big stuff, my financial adviser told me not to sweat the small things like credit in□uires or incorrect dates. I didn't listen. Instead, I disputed everything, thinking every point mattered. If a creditor pulled my credit without my permission, I disputed it. If my credit card company reported my balance higher than it should have been six months ago, I disputed it. In total, I raised my credit score 88 points by disputing every little error.

A 'closed-door' impeachment process: Three questions.

By law, the credit bureaus must investigate valid claims and remove inaccurate information, but if you run into trouble, complain to the Consumer Financial Protection Bureau.

20. Add missing accounts

Once I cleaned up my credit history, I started looking for ways to build it. I did this by looking for credit lines that could have been included in my file, but weren't. For example, I've had a cell phone in my name for 10 years, but those payments didn't appear on my credit report. So I made a list of every company I paid monthly, contacted the companies, and asked them to report my payment history to the credit bureaus. Below are the types of companies that were willing to report on my behalf:

Wireless provider

Cable and Internet provider

Utility company

Telephone company

Keep in mind, however, that no company is re□uired to report your payments, on-time or not, and many utility companies won't. So when you approach companies like those above, you're asking for a favor, not making a demand. To learn more about utilities reporting to credit agencies, see "The Movement to Put Utility Payments on Credit Reports" from the New York Times.

21. Pay down your highest balance

If you're carrying balances on several credit cards, it's tempting to pay off your smaller balances first, thinking that will motivate you to attack the larger debts. But if you're trying to boost your credit score quickly, you should start by paying off the credit card with the lowest available credit limit. For example, say you have two credit cards. One credit card has a $1,600 limit with a $400 balance, which means 25 percent of your available credit is being used. The second card has a $1,000 limit with an $800 balance, meaning 80 percent of your available credit is being utilized. In this case, the second credit card is doing worse damage to your credit score because of its higher utilization ratio. Pay it off first and your credit score will improve faster.

22. Pay by your report date, not your due date

Obviously, if you want good credit, you'll pay your bills on or before their due date. But if you want to maintain a high credit score, it may be a good idea to pay some earlier — before balances are reported.

For example, say your credit card company reports your balance to credit reporting agencies every month on the 10th, but your bill is due on the 20th. At the first of the month you charge $5,000, but pay your bill in full on the 20th. As far as you're concerned, you're not carrying a balance: you got your bill and paid it by the due date. But if someone checks your credit on the 15th, the credit reporting agency will report you have a $5,000 balance.

I called my creditor and asked what day they reported my payment history, which turned out to be a week earlier than my due date. From that moment on, I've made my credit card payment before the reporting date, not the due date. That means if my credit is pulled, I always show a zero balance on my plastic.

23. Blend your credit (BOUNUS)

Three years ago I applied for an auto loan and was denied because I didn't have a good mix of credit types. Lenders like to see that you can manage different types of credit and handle multiple accounts at once, but I only had two major credit cards. So I applied for a small installment loan (one with fixed payments and an established due date) from my bank and paid it back over 12 months. Adding installment credit to my already established revolving (credit card) credit lines boosted my credit score by about 30 points.

24. Keep using your credit cards (BONUS)

Several years ago I heard a nugget of financial wisdom, "When you're rebuilding your credit, tear up your credit cards." Now, if you're struggling to manage your spending habits, this is sound advice, but if you're just trying to raise your credit score, cutting up your credit cards can be more harmful than helpful. For example, I spent nearly a year trying to improve my credit score. During that time, I put a small amount on both of my credit cards each month and then made sure I paid the balance on time. While I was disputing errors and working on building up new credit, I was also adding 12 months of on-time payments to my existing credit score.

The bottom line – every month counts. If you can manage your credit cards, keep using them.

25. Ask for a credit line increase (BONUS)

Your credit utilization ratio, mentioned briefly above, is something lenders use to see how you're managing your available credit. For example, if you have a $15,000 available credit limit and a $400 balance, you're utilizing little of your available credit, so you look strong. If you carry that same $400 balance on a card with a $500 credit limit, you've borrowed nearly as much as you can, making you appear more risky.

While paying off your balance is the best solution, I found a □uick fix that improved my credit score while I was paying off debt. I simply called my credit card company and asked if they would increase my available credit limit. They agreed and raised my limit, which lowered my overall credit utilization ratio and gave me a 15 point boost.

Once your credit score is in the prime range, do everything you can to protect it. When you have several late payments, collection accounts, and charge-offs, one mistake won't hurt you too much, but when you have a near-perfect credit score, even one late payment will cause a big drop. Make sure you pay your bills on time, don't max out your credit cards, and never co-sign for someone else's debt. If the co-signer doesn't pay the bill, your credit could end up worse than ever before.

NEW HOPE CREDIT SOLUTIONS LLC helps by giving you credit for the utility and mobile phone bills you're already paying. Until now, those payments did not positively impact your score.

This service is completely free and can boost your credit scores fast by using your own positive payment history. It can also help those with poor or limited credit situations. Other services such as credit repair may cost you up to thousands and only help remove inaccuracies from your credit report.

CONCLUSION

Your credit score—a three-digit number lenders use to help them decide how likely it is they'll be repaid on time if they grant you a credit card or loan—is an important factor in your financial life. The higher your scores, the more likely you are to ☐ualify for loans and credit cards at the most favorable terms, which will save you money.

If your credit history is not where you want it to be, you're not alone. NEW HOPE CREDIT SOLUTIONS LLC is with you.

ABOUT US

 New Hope Credit Solutions LLC is a credit score improvement company operating out of New York City. We are a company that focuses on helping individuals and businesses getting errors removed from their credit profiles. We have an efficient management system and a team that makes use of modern and efficient methods to dispute erroneous credit claims and help our clients improve their credit score significantly. Our founder and CEO is an avid entrepreneur and industry expert with over 20 years of experience in Sales, marketing, and finance. He is a firm believer in putting family first. He is also a published author with a burning desire to help people achieve financial freedom through credit repair restoration and funding.

Our Mission Statement

To give extreme value and personal attention with understanding, care and trust.

Contact New Hope Credit Solutions LLC on:

https://www.facebook.com/newhopecreditsolutions

https://www.instagram.com/newhopecred/

www.ingramcontent.com/pod-product-compliance
Lightning Source LLC
Chambersburg PA
CBHW070520220526
45467CB00002B/768